dennis christopher jorenetta

THE RUSSIAN REVOLUTION

by Nicolas Berdyaev

Ann Arbor Paperbacks for the Study of Communism and Marxism
The University of Michigan Press

Second printing 1966
First edition as an Ann Arbor Paperback 1961
All rights reserved
First published in 1931 by Sheed and Ward
Published in the United States of America by
The University of Michigan Press and simultaneously
in Toronto, Canada, by Ambassador Books Limited
Manufactured in the United States of America

CONTENTS

I

RUSSIAN RELIGIOUS PSYCHOLOGY AND COMMUNISTIC ATHEISM

THE Russian Revolution has interested the whole world in Russia and the Russian people. The peoples of the West are uneasy about the Communist experiment, accompanied as it is by a forced implanting of atheism such as the world has never yet known—an experiment carried on in a vast country which is little known to, and little understood by, the West. What must be of great interest is the psychological problem : How was it possible for Holy Russia to be turned into an arsenal of militant atheism ? How is it that a people who are religious by their very structure and live exclusively by faith have proved to be such a fruitful field for anti-religious propaganda ? To explain that, to understand Russian *anti-religious* psychology, one must have an insight into the *religious* psychology of the Russian people.

[handwritten margin note: psychological problem]

[handwritten margin note: counters Colin Wilson's thesis of non-religious]

i

The nineteenth century saw the advent of an original type of Russian, different in spiritual

1

structure from that of mediæval Muscovite Russia, and it is this type which gives us the key to the militant atheism of the Russian Revolution. In Russia it was a century of thought and word, in which the structure of the Russian soul was first realised and expressed ; in which creative art and thought have left memorials through which we can study the religious and anti-religious tendencies of Russian psychology. But the roots of this soul-structure we are to study lie embedded in the tragic history of our past, and above all in the religious schism (*Raskol*) within the Russian Church of the seventeenth century, the effects of which are still at work in our own day. The *Raskol* is a characteristic and decisive phenomenon of Russian history, and we have not deflected from its orbit. Russians are, by their very psychology, inclined to become *raskolniki* (schismatics).

The historic religious schism is not to be explained merely by the fact that a considerable portion of the Russian people and clergy in the times before Peter the Great were grossly ignorant and identified ritual with dogma. The struggle was carried on not merely to preserve the ancient rites, the letter of the law, in all their purity. Deeper motives, to be found in the psychological history of the Russian people, were in action. They had long been moved by

2

the feeling of a messianic mission. It found expression in the fifteenth century, in the teaching of the monk Philothey concerning Moscow, " the Third Rome." Byzantium had fallen, and the only Orthodox Empire left in the world, according to Philothey, was the Russian ; the Russian nation, alone on the earth, was the depositary of true Orthodox faith ; all the outer Christian world had tarnished its purity. The idea of an Orthodox Empire became the Russians' central idea—a messianic idea.

When Greek influence showed itself in the correction of the service-books and the alteration of the rites, this was taken as a betrayal of the Orthodox Empire, the civil power and the hierarchy of the Church. Religious and national sentiment were as closely wedded as in the consciousness of the ancient Jews. When the Patriarch Nikon fell under Greek influence, he seemed a traitor. Antichrist had penetrated into the Orthodox Empire, into State and Church. The hierarchy was corrupted. The true Church went out into the desert and hid beneath the earth. The Orthodox Empire, like the town of Kitesh *, became an invisible one. The *raskolniki* took refuge in the forests and hid

---

* According to legend, the " Shining Town " of Kitesh, rather than fall a prey to the Mongols, sank to the bottom of a lake. (Translator's note.)

from persecution. The more fanatical and exalted among them burned themselves to death ; the sect of " self-burners " is a typically Russian phenomenon.

"priestlessness"

Another extreme form of the *Raskol* is *bezpopovstvo* (" priestlessness "), which rejects every sort of hierarchy, has a strong apocalyptic and eschatological tendency, and is nihilistic in its attitude to the structure of the Church, to the State, and to culture.

nihilism

Russian Nihilism and the apocalyptic strain in the Russian character are connected, and their connection shows itself in the extreme forms of the schismatic spirit. Nihilistic and apocalyptic tendencies, hankering after spiritual nakedness, refusal of the processes of history and of cultural values, expectancy of some final catastrophe, are deeply rooted in the psychology of the *Raskol*. Its extreme left wing brought forth a multitude of sects. The monarchism of the Old-Believers developed into anarchism. The psychology of the *Raskol*, a divorce between the Church's people and her rulers, between the common people and the cultured class, grew more and more strong and violent. The reform of Peter the Great greatly increased it. Popular feeling saw in Peter's reform, or, rather, in his revolution, an act of violence against the people's soul, and answered it by creating the

left-wing → factionalism & sects [4]
right-wing [monarchists] → anarchism

legend that he was Antichrist. Henceforth the Orthodox Christian Empire is taken as having finally disappeared from the visible world, and the realm of Antichrist takes its place. Imperial Russia, soaked in Western civilisation, is no longer the Orthodox Empire in the strict sense of the word. An attitude of aloofness and suspicion towards the authorities grows up. The Russian religious messianic idea remains, but it settles into a profound divorce from its actual surroundings. Orthodoxy, bound up with the dominant Church but opposed to Protestant or " enlightening " influences, kept much in common with the Old-Believers and *raskolniki*. Apocalyptic feelings, connected with the awaiting of Antichrist, are very strong among the people, and they come to light also in currents of religious thought among the cultured classes, in Russian writers and thinkers. And these tendencies remain as psychological forces, but in a secularised form, in movements which are divorced from Christian religious consciousness. Thus a schismatic and eschatological disposition is the fundamental psychological fact of the Russian nineteenth century ; it will express itself both in a religious way and in an anti-religious (an inverted religious) way.

The Russian *intelligentsia* of the nineteenth century was a class of intellectual schismatics,

5

an intellectual *Raskol*. It lived in disagreement with the present, with Imperial Russia; it looked either to an ideal past, idealising the Russia before Peter, or to an ideal future, an idealised West. It did not feel the successes of the Russian State to be its own successes. Lack of any foundation or root in real life was a characteristic feature of the Russian soul in the nineteenth century. And with it went a great independence and boldness of thought. All intellectuals, whether Slavophil or Occidentalist, refused their own time as a period in which the vocation of the Russian people was not fulfilled; and such a negative attitude to contemporary life is a revolutionary element. The Slavophils looked to the past, to Russia as it was before Peter the Great, while the Occidentalists looked to the West; but both former Russia and Western Europe were dreams, not realities.

When the Occidentalist, Herzen, found himself in the West and saw its commonness, he underwent a most painful disenchantment; he inveighed against the *bourgeois* spirit of the West, which has always revolted Russians. As for the Slavophils, they were convinced monarchists, but the monarchy of Nicholas I disgusted them. Russian thought in the nineteenth century, fed on German romanticism, adopted its themes and developed them in its own way. It was

6

thought without roots ; and this defect was a national feature ; it could only dream of some organised form of culture.

In the spiritual fabric of the cultured intellectual class of Russia in the nineteenth century a number of features typical of later developments appeared : divorce from contemporary life ; consciousness of the gulf that separated it as a class from the people and from the rulers ; eschatological feeling as a spiritual disposition independent of religious faith, sometimes religious and sometimes social ; expectancy of a catastrophic end ; maximalism ; little understanding of hierarchical degrees and of the gradual nature of historical developments ; a tendency to deny the value of the relative, and to turn it into something absolute ; an inclination towards opposite extremes ; a curious kind of asceticism ; contempt of worldly goods and *bourgeois* virtues ; a crying demand for the actual attainment of justice in human life, above all in social life. One can recognise these features in the most contradictory tendencies.

The Russian soul of the nineteenth century was a suffering soul brought to the point of self-torture. Compassion for human suffering was the fundamental theme of its literature—a spiritual disposition that fed upon the painful aspects of serfdom. It was essentially a non-

7

acceptance of suffering ; not a refusal to suffer, but a refusal to admit that there was any meaning in it. Now, this Russian suffering and compassion had two sources : in some it came from consciousness of guilt, contrition, an uneasy conscience ; in others from a feeling of offence, resentment, a revolt of the oppressed. And the basic phenomenon which we have to notice is that we have here *a transposition of religious motives and religious psychology into a non-religious or anti-religious sphere, into the region of social problems, so that the spiritual energy of religion flows into social channels, which thereby take on a religious character,* and become a breeding-ground for a peculiar form of social idolatry. Creative social energy was not free to find its realisation in the conditions of actual Russian life, it was not directed into actual social construction ; it entered into its own self, modified the texture of the soul, elicited a passionate visionary social idealism, and accumulated an explosive force in the depths of the subconscious mind. No one had a more profound insight than Dostoievsky into the fact that Russian Socialism was not a political but a religious question, the question of God, of immortality and the radical reconstruction of all human life. Socialism, broadly speaking, was the dominant religious faith of most of the nineteenth-century Russian *intelli-*

[margin handwritten note: transition of "pro-religion" to "social Religion"]

gentsia. It determined all moral judgments. It was above all a matter of sentiment. The Russians' interpretation of Saint Simon, Proudhon and Karl Marx was a religious one ; they took to materialism also in the same religious spirit. Dostoievsky revealed the religious psychology and religious dialectics of Russian Nihilism and revolutionary Socialism. And once one has understood the basis of Russian Nihilism, and recognised it as an original product of the Russian spirit, one is able to grasp the source and basis of the militant atheistic element in Russian Communism.

nihilism & the russian spirit

ii

Russian Nihilism was directed, at its origins, by religious motives which concealed a perverted religious psychology. Russians became Nihilists through a kind of love of truth and justice. It was Bielinsky, the Russian Orthodox literary critic and publicist of the 'forties, that came in the latter period of his life to hold the philosophy which laid the basis of Russian Nihilism and nihilistic Socialism. A typical intellectual *raskolnik*, Bielinsky searched for truth throughout his life and became a Nihilist and an atheist for love of justice and the welfare of the people and of humanity. In his person

9

the idealism of the 'forties underwent a crisis, Russian derivatives from Schelling and Hegel came to an end, and the consciousness of the *intelligentsia* was brought into contact with social realities.

Bielinsky deliberately plunged into those realities in the name of an idealistic longing for justice and hatred of falsehood. He began life as an idealist and a romantic, in love with " the sublime and the beautiful," and ended it as a realist and an atheist. The crisis began by his protesting against the absoluteness of Hegel's spirit, against everything general and universal, against all abstract ideas, in the name of concrete human personality, with its joys and sorrows. And then a most interesting psychological process took place. Bielinsky passionately rejected the abstract notions of idealism, but he settled on living concrete human personality only for a brief moment, and then set out at once to subject it to a new set of abstract ideas which seemed to him to be realistic—the ideal of social justice and the welfare of mankind. He threw his passionate nature into a love of humanity which he himself called " Marat's love." He declared that he was ready to cut off the heads of a large section of mankind in order to make the rest happy, and so anticipated Bolshevik morals. " If I were the Tsar," he cried, " I would be a tyrant." His motto was Socialism or death. Obligatory happiness for everyone ; suffering has no right to exist.

Bielinsky became a citizen of the universe ; he was completely possessed by the idea of atheistic Socialism. His love of justice and humanity turned him into an atheist, with atheism as his religious faith. " I am a terrible man," he said, " when some mystical folly gets into my head." The average Russian is just such a " terrible man " ; his idea, when he is an atheist, is just such a " mystical folly." In Bielinsky, however, there still remains a veneration for Christ as a friend of the poor and the fallen, who preached a religion of compassion. Harnack has remarked that the ideas of Marcionism are native to the Russians. It is true that the Russian atheism of the " earthly idealists," as they are sometimes called to distinguish them from the " heavenly," is inspired by tendencies akin to Marcionism ; it arises chiefly out of their being tortured by the problem of evil, injustice and suffering. But Marcion, though he revolted against God, Creator of the World, the God of the Old Testament, as an evil Demiurge, because He created a world full of evil and suffering, admitted an unseen, distant God, Father of Jesus Christ, the Saviour and Redeemer of the world. Russian

11

atheism rejected every kind of God, because to admit God was to justify evil, injustice and suffering and give in to them. Evil was considered above all as suffering. Bielinsky had already sharply underlined the problem of how " the little child's poor tears " are a necessary condition of creation—the problem which Dostoievsky later put into the mouth of Ivan in *The Brothers Karamazov*. He will not accept a world whose creation is accompanied by the sufferings of human beings. He wants to destroy that world and create a new one where suffering does not exist. God created an unjust world full of suffering, and therefore He must be rejected for moral reasons.

Russian nihilistic and atheistic Socialism arises out of compassion for suffering personality and defence of it against society. The purely Russian Socialism of the so-called *narodniki* (" lovers of the people ") was individualistic at its origin ; one still notices that in the 'seventies in N. Mikhailovsky, who built up a whole theory of " the struggle for individuality." But Russian atheistic Socialism ended by rejecting personality and dealing with it cruelly and mercilessly. That is the fatal outcome of its inner logical process. One sees this in Bielinsky, with his readiness to inflict great suffering in order to abolish suffering, and destroy human

persons for the benefit of human personality.
For " Marat's love " of mankind is always like
that. It begins by protesting against the
" universal " that oppresses and tortures personality, and ends up by proclaiming a new
" universal "—love of humanity ; not, however, the love of living human persons, but love
of the *idea* of humanity ; love of something " far
off," the abstract idea of justice and a perfect
social order. And this new " universal " turns
living human personality into its own tool and
instrument, denying its absolute value and
interior life. Compassion turns into cruelty,
freedom into compulsion and violence ; defence
of personality against the tyranny of society
leads to extreme social despotism. Such is the
fate of an atheism which seemed to be determined by noble spiritual motives. And that is
what disclosed itself in the Russian Nihilism of
the 'sixties ; it was a paradox combining in
itself a struggle for personal freedom and an
extreme violation of personality by social utilitarianism, a denial of its right to individual life
and creation. Nihilism does not understand
the mystery of the Cross, the meaning of suffering, and that is why it fails as a religion.

Russian Nihilism of the early 'sixties was
largely founded by priests' sons, who had been
believers in their childhood and were brought

up in the school of Orthodoxy. The most striking examples are Dobroliubov and Cherny-shevsky, both of whom, like all our " en-lighteners," were literary critics and publicists. Chernyshevsky was also an economist. Dobro-liubov's diary, which was published, shows in what type of soul Nihilism and anti-religious feeling can grow up. His childish, youthful soul astounds one by its religiousness, its earnest faith, its moral purity, its seriousness, its severe ascetic character ; and it remained such to the very end of his life. He died very young (Russian Nihilism of the 'sixties was, indeed, above all a Youth Movement, a revolt of young souls ; Pisarev, too, the most pugnacious and brilliant of Russian Nihilists, was quite a young man when he died). As a child, Dobro-liubov was tortured by the experience of sin. His conscience reproached him with his most insignificant misdeeds, such as eating too much jam or sleeping too long ; he had a passion for purity. He loved his parents, especially his mother, in a most touching way. Though still in his early childhood, he was wounded by the decadent, unspiritual life of the Russian clergy. He was thunderstruck by the death of his parents, especially of his mother, taking it as a manifestation of evil in the world. He lost his faith because he could not stand the scandal

14

and injustice of the world, or the baseness of his Orthodox Christian surroundings. He wanted light, and he seemed to be surrounded by the kingdom of darkness. He decided that man himself must bring light into this dark unjust world, and he became a Nihilist " enlightener " (*prosvetitel*).

Russian *prosvetitelstvo* (self-devotion to the " enlightenment " of the people) generally takes the form of Nihilism, and in this the radicalism and maximalism of the Russian makes itself felt. Dobroliubov's life was short and joyless. His Nihilism was directed by nothing but noble and pure spiritual motives ; he could not see the corrupting results of Nihilism. Dobroliubov did not understand the meaning of the Cross ; he suffered but did not bear the Cross.

Chernyshevsky, the chief theorist of Russian Nihilism in the 'sixties and of atheistic Socialism, was also a man of the clerical class, a priest's son. There was an ascetic element, inherited from Orthodoxy, in his mental outlook. He was an honest, pure, disinterested, self-sacrificing man, who spent nineteen years as a convict for an insignificant political offence and bore the trial courageously. His novel, *What's to be Done ?* in which he proposes a Nihilist social Utopia, is very weak as a work of art, but it

15

contains strong ascetic and moral elements. The hero, Rakhmetov, sleeps on nails so as to harden his character ! Early Nihilism was characterised by the quest of truth at all costs, a protest against every conventional lie and hypocrisy ; it was especially a denudation, a throwing away of all veils and garments, a belief that, once that was done, the truth of life would be revealed. The naïve materialism that the Russian Nihilists professed like a religious faith was determined chiefly by moral, one may even say ascetic, considerations. They held that any sort of idealistic or spiritual metaphysics was an unlawful luxury, a mental debauch, a forgetfulness of the sufferings of the common people. It was their duty to live in poverty and be satisfied with bare necessities. Bukharev, one of the most remarkable and original of Russian theologians in the nineteenth century, appreciated Chernyshevsky's book *What's to be Done ?* very highly from the moral point of view. He saw in it certain true, though unconscious, Christian elements. The youth Pisarev made a real massacre of æsthetics and art, and rejected Pushkin ; he did so for ascetic reasons. Æsthetics are a useless and inadmissible luxury. The only art that can be allowed is art that serves the actual needs of mankind. The thinking realist, as Pisarev called his ideal of human personality, must turn to unbeautified reality, and, above all, free himself from all illusions and self-deceit, from every mental or artistic luxury.

The Nihilism of the 'sixties had already brought forth the main themes that operate and triumph in the Bolshevik Revolution : hatred of all religion, mysticism, metaphysics and pure art, as things which deflect energy from the creation of a better social order ; substitution of social utilitarianism for all absolute morality ; exclusive domination of natural science and political economy, together with suspicion of the humanities ; recognition of the labourers, workmen and peasants, as the only real men ; oppression of interior personal life by the social principle and social utility ; the Utopia of a perfect social structure. Perfection in life is to be attained not by changing man, but by changing society. It is understood first and foremost as freedom from suffering and the advent of happiness.

The demands of Russian Nihilism entered into Communism and are being executed by it. Here we have to deal with the spiritual sources of Russian Nihilism, and show up its fundamental self-contradiction. As a peculiar production of the Russian spirit, a Russian spiritual sickness, it could only be experienced by a soul that had grown up on the spiritual soil of

Orthodoxy, but had lost its faith. As in our popular schism, so also in our intellectual Nihilism, one is conscious of an ascetic denial of the world and of culture that proceeds from the Orthodox religious character. The gradualness of history is foreign to Orthodox consciousness ; Orthodoxy is the least evolutionary, the most eschatological form of Christianity. Doubts as to whether culture is justifiable are a traditional theme of Russian religious and social thought. Is not culture perhaps bought at too dear a price ? Is it not foreign to the common people ? Does it not transform real life into something false, conventional, artificial, illusory ? Purely Russian questions, these. *Nihilism, at its sources and in its purest form, is asceticism without grace ; asceticism not in the name of God, but in the name of the future welfare of mankind, in the name of a perfect society.* And this graceless, Godless asceticism urges men to perform deeds of prowess, to make sacrifices, to lay down their lives. It will not be reconciled with the injustice and suffering of the world, but desires its end and ruin, and the advent of a new world. Its psychology is eschatological.

With this graceless asceticism, Nihilism is torn by a fundamental contradiction : it begins by wanting to emancipate personality and free it from the slavery of social surroundings, with

their norms and rules, traditions and preju-
dices, and yet it finally enslaves the human
person to social utility and the interests of
society ; it denies the right of personality to
lead its own spiritual and creative life ; it
rejects religion, philosophy, art, morality as
qualitative contents of personal life, and throws
down all values that exalt personality. And it
is obliged to do so, because it considers human
personality to be a mere product of social surroundings, and denies its spiritual nature. It
rejects morality for moral reasons. It professes
the grossest utilitarianism, yet it is moralist
through and through. It ends up in moralistic
social utilitarianism. Now, that means the complete subjection of personality to society. Personal moral conscience is done away with and
replaced by the moral conscience of society, the
group, the movement, the party. This comes
out with extraordinary force in Communism.
The social motives in Communism proved to be
stronger than those of personal emancipation ;
stronger than the yearning for personal perfection and truth, which is a considerable force in
Pisarev's Nihilism. Nihilism denied all spiritual
and cultural values, but it recognised one value
as supreme, the value of social truth, justice, the
welfare of the people, the happiness of the lower
working classes. It is immoral to think of any-

thing except that higher value ; everything must be sacrificed to it. The conflict of religious faith and scientific knowledge, which played such a large part in the rise of infidelity in the West, plays quite a secondary one in Russia. Russian infidelity, Russian militant atheism, has moral and social motives at its basis. The Russian soul is troubled not so much by any conflict between Christianity and science as by that between it and social truth, by the fact that Christianity backs up social untruth. It is wounded, above all, by the conventional, false and hypocritical rhetoric indulged in by Christians. Science itself becomes, for Russian Nihilism and atheism, an object of religious faith and idolatry, and this only confirms the fact that it is not a question of mere objective science.

Vladimir Solovyev expressed the fundamental paradox of Russian Nihilism thus : " Man has evolved out of a monkey—therefore it is our duty to love one another." To profess the theory of man's origin from the monkeys, and profess it in the grossest manner, becomes a social duty. If you profess the truth that God created man after His own image and likeness, you will probably be in favour of serfdom, a defender of social injustice ; you will justify social evil and be an enemy of the working people. Darwinism, like materialism, has become a necessary part of the Communist catechism. As a matter of fact, it is in no way favourable to Communism, and rather justifies the capitalist system. But for Russian Nihilists and atheists, science has become a catechism that lays down an obligatory doctrine to be held by faith.

In the 'seventies the extremes and roughness of Russian Nihilism were toned down, and social preoccupations finally got the upper hand in it. It was a time when the *intelligentsia* went out to the simple working people, to the peasantry, to work for their welfare and their emancipation. It witnessed the final formation of Russian *narodnichestvo*—the belief that the real truth of life is to be found in the working people (*narod*), especially in the peasantry. But the intellectual *narodniki* were divorced from the people's faith, from Orthodoxy, and they infected them with atheism. The left wing of the Russian *intelligentsia*, Nihilist in its views on religion and philosophy, Socialist and "a lover of the people," was made up of people partly from the class of nobles, and partly from various other branches of society, generally from the lower classes. But the psychology of these two classes was different. For the nobles it was generally the result of a stricken conscience, repentance for social sin ; for the others, a matter of honour and indignation, a revolt of the oppressed. Mikhailovsky gave up fighting for his own rights and cried out, " The peasant is whipped, let me be whipped too." A characteristic feature of Russian atheistic Socialism and *narodnichestvo*, was an extraordinary capacity for self-sacrifice. Its adepts, the best among them at least, denied themselves the pleasures of their own temporal life ; they went lightheartedly to prison, to forced labour, to the scaffold, without the consolation of belief in an eternal life hereafter—a very interesting psychological phenomenon. They were people who held earthly good and happiness to be the only object of life, and yet they were prepared to make sacrifices and undergo suffering in order to further that end, which they personally had no hopes of attaining in their lifetime. And so they were called " earthly idealists." The comparison with contemporary Christians was by no means a favourable one. The greater mass of decadent Christians of the nineteenth century gave little proof of capacity for self-sacrifice ; they clung to the good things of this world and consoled themselves with those of the next. This did much to strengthen anti-Christian and anti-religious feeling. Religious and philosophical spiritualism and idealism were associated with

22

injustice in earthly living, with practical materialism. A justice that was put away into heaven seemed a hindrance to the realisation of justice on earth. The Christian martyrs, saints and ascetics were forgotten ; they were far away in the remote past. Contemporary Christianity was too much used as a means to earthly goods and interests. Denunciation of the untruth, falsehood and hypocrisy of so-called Christian society inspired and nourished antireligious psychology. The unworthiness and sinfulness of Christians became a victorious argument against Christianity itself.

It is worthy of note that the Anarchist revolt against the false contemporary world, which called itself Christian, came from men of the upper aristocratic class of the Russian nobility. Such is the Anarchism of Bakunin, of Prince Kropotkin, and the peculiar religious Anarchism of Count Leo Tolstoy. Bakunin combined Anarchism with militant atheism ; he rebelled against God, the Creator of the world, as against Satan, and he saw in Him the source of power and government, that is, of the greatest evil of life on earth. His Anarchism has an almost mystical note in it ; it is a kind of religious phenomenon. The old Russian messianic idea, purely religious in its basis, rises up again in a new way in Bakunin. The Russian and

Slavonic world has the great mission of lighting a vast fire which is to burn up the old sinful world. This passion for destruction is a creative passion. Out of the ash-heap, out of the ruins of the old world, a new world will arise, free and beautiful. This revolutionary, messianic idea of Bakunin has found its way into Russian Communism, which believes that the Russian people are to send forth a light that will illuminate the *bourgeois* darkness of Western Europe.

Tolstoy, though no atheist, was a kind of religious Russian Nihilist. His appearance was only possible on the spiritual background of Russian Orthodoxy. He also separated himself in an anarchical and nihilistic spirit from the world of falsehood and untruth, revolted against its history and culture, and overturned all its values. He searched passionately for true life, and in its name he yearned for denudation, for the rejection of all earthly trappings. Divine justice is only to be discovered in Nature, in life according to Nature. Tolstoy preached a Christianity of his own. Psychologically it still contained many strong Orthodox and ascetic elements, but in his impassioned and indignant criticism of historical Christianity and the Church, with its dogmas and sacraments, one often comes across the same themes and argu-

24

ments that occur in anti-religious propaganda. He repents of the social and cultural sin and falsehood on which the so-called Christian world is founded.

It is typical of Russian psychology that the Russian soul has suffered bitterly from the crisis of culture and been inclined to criticise it. And so it rebels against religion and the Church, in so far as they have become part of culture and submitted to its laws and norms. Not only the Russian anti-religious movements of the nineteenth and twentieth centuries, but also the religious movements revolted against " historical " Christianity, that is, against Christianity as it appears and acts in history and so submits to the untruth, violence, injustice and evil that rule history. We have here a very characteristic Russian tendency, which sometimes took the form of a radical rejection of Christianity and religion, and sometimes that of a yearning for some sort of pure Christianity unspoilt by history. Russian thought was preoccupied by the philosophy of history, but the relativity of history disgusted its absolute consciousness. Every earthly city is evil, unjust, relative, subject to the prince of this world. Christians have no lasting city, they seek the city that is to come. And the quest of that city is shared even by those Russian souls which have denied God in its name, out of protest against the earthly city full of evil and injustice. Russian atheists seek the Kingdom of God upon earth, but without God and against Him. The psychology of Russian atheism is a survival of ancient gnostic and anarchical ideas : the Creator of the world is an evil God, who made an evil, unjust world full of suffering, and therefore every power on earth is an evil, satanic power, belonging to the prince of this world, and to fight injustice is to fight an evil God, the author of the world. These ideas already appear in the extreme forms of the Russian *Raskol* and the Russian sects. They operate also in the revolutionary *intelligentsia*, but in its consciousness they are combined with the most superficial of Western materialist doctrines. Russian atheism, in its most profound forms, may be expressed in the following paradox : God must be denied, in order that the Kingdom of God may come on earth. In Russian religious psychology there was always a strong prophetic element. Torn up from its religious roots and perverted, it remains in Russian atheism with its social basis. That atheism comes, above all, from having forgotten that Christ, our God, Himself suffered and was sacrificed for us.

26

iii

But what is most interesting of all in our subject is the way Russian Nihilism and atheism passed into Communism. In the new psychological phenomenon of the Communists' militant atheism we can watch the fatal logic of that Nihilism and atheism which are connected with the Russian quest of external social justice. The Russian Communists' atheism is quite a different psychological phenomenon, connected with quite another soul-structure. Why did the Russian soul, with its compassionate love of mankind and its hankering for justice, absorb the teaching of Marx, which would seem to be so foreign to it? Dostoievsky foresaw a great deal, but Marxism was not yet within his ken. He only knew French Socialism. With the victory of the Revolution, Russian atheism and anti-religious sentiment enter a completely new phase.

Karl Marx, who began by following L. Feuerbach in his views on religion, later declared that it was " opium for the people " (he uses that expression in his essay on Hegel's *Philosophy of Law*), and considered that religious faith was the greatest hindrance to the emancipation of the proletariat, and therefore of all mankind. Poor weak man has a strong, rich

God, and gives up to Him all his wealth and strength. The struggle against God means that man will attain wealth and strength ; once he is rich and strong he will have no need of God. Religion transports the realisation of man's welfare into an illusory, imaginary world of unreality, and so hinders its really being attained ; it weakens man's activity and paralyses his determination to organise social life. Religion holds out illusory consolations and therefore it sanctions injustice, poverty and weakness in earthly life. Heaven is the arch-enemy that prevents earth from being set right. The tone of Marxian atheism is quite different from that of traditional Russian atheism, which had included strong elements of compassion, pity and a sort of asceticism, whereas Marxian atheism is chiefly concerned with strength—the power of organised society. Religious faith must be plucked from the heart of man and the idea of God destroyed, in order that human society may become powerful, human life be definitely organised and rationalised, and that the final victory over the elemental powers of Nature and the elemental irrational forces in human society may become possible. The Marxian type of atheism is not moved at all by pity ; on the contrary, it is pitiless. In order to procure power and riches for the social collectivity it proclaims ruthless cruelty towards men. There is no humanitarian element left in it. It comes from Feuerbach, but it goes one further than him and rejects his religion of humanity. It was not in the name of man that Marx raised the standard of revolt, but in the name of the mightiness of a new deity, the social collectivity. He is not so much moved by pity for the suffering humiliated proletariat, longing to alleviate its sufferings and liberate it from humiliation, as by the idea of the coming might and power of the proletariat, the future messiah destined to organise an earthly empire. The pathos of Marx is, above all, one of power ; it is full of strength and longs for conquest ; it is a victorious psychology. He wants man, as a social and socialised being, to become a powerful organiser and constructor.

Already at the end of the nineteenth century a strong Marxist movement grew up in Russia, entered into battle against the old " people-loving " Socialism, and essentially modified the outlook and tendency of the radical Russian *intelligentsia*. The intellectual elements prevailed in it over the sentimental. And at the beginning of the twentieth century Russian Marxism split up. The more cultured Marxists went through a spiritual crisis and became the founders of an idealist and religious movement, while the majority began to prepare the advent of Communism. And so we come to the chief psychological riddle : Why did the Marxian type of atheism, apparently so uncongenial, win the day in Russia ? Why did the Russian Revolution adopt the Marxian creed? Why did it become the obligatory catechism of the Communist Party ?

The Marxian type of atheism, inspired by the will to rule and the pathos of power, gained the upper hand in Russia when the Revolution was victorious ; the compassionate people, yearning for justice, the oppressed and the persecuted, became masters of the situation, and themselves changed into oppressors and persecutors. Compassionate atheism, the atheism of weakness, changed into a domineering atheism, an atheism of power. Suffering rejects its own meaning and wants to turn into happiness. A psychological metamorphosis took place. The expression on Russian faces changed. A sort of new anthropological type appeared, that had grown up and formed in the War, and triumphed in the Revolution. The victorious, organising atheist made his appearance. The suffering soul-structure of the old Russian revolutionaries turned out to be absolutely useless and inapplicable to the new conditions and the new epoch. And the old revolutionaries, formed in the time of oppression and persecution, underwent a spiritual re-birth. Communism made a natural selection of a particular kind of soul-structure. The young men came straight into life with a new mentality. They had a psychology of the victorious, a psychology of the members of one class that have conquered those of another, which reminds one of the attitude of races and nations that have conquered other races and nations. A conqueror who triumphs and is conscious of his strength has a different psychology from that of a weak, oppressed, enslaved man, who pities the weak and the oppressed. The spiritual outlook of men who seek truth and revolt against dominant untruth, differs from that of men who look upon themselves as the bearers of truth that has conquered and dominates. Old Russian Nihilism and atheism was born either of repentance and compassion on the part of the privileged cultured classes or of offence and resentment on the part of the oppressed. Neither of the two felt themselves to be victorious. The penitent revolted noblemen deserted the governing class, but they left their dominant position and lost their power over life. It was they who came into power in the victorious Revolution. The dominant part in it was played by those who had been offended

and oppressed, and the resentment that characterised them took on new forms. The type of
the avenger comes in. Atheism becomes an
atheism of revenge, it persecutes religion, closes
churches, oppresses the clergy. The avenger
considers that he was offended and oppressed
because of the domination of religious beliefs
that maintained that offence and oppression.
When an offended and oppressed man, whose
mental outlook is one of resentment, comes into
rule and power, it is difficult for him to act
nobly and magnanimously ; nobility and
magnanimity are aristocratic virtues that
flourish in souls free from resentment.

In former Russia the people, especially the
peasant and middle classes, were more believing
in and truer to Orthodoxy than the upper
classes, the nobility, which had come under
the influence of the free-thinking philosophy of
enlightenment and Voltairianism in the eighteenth century and the *intelligentsia*. At the
Revolution the idea of enlightened philosophy,
which in Russia always inclines to Nihilism,
came down among the common people and, in
a very vulgarised form, took possession of the
labouring and peasant youth. It is a process in
the popular sphere analogous to that which
took place in the *intelligentsia* of the 'sixties.
But the psychological difference is enormous.

Among the masses, atheism and Nihilism mean a protest against the beliefs which, as their consciousness, worked upon by anti-religious propaganda, teaches, held them in slavery. In Communism we now find an anti-religious psychology different from that of former Nihilism.

Between Bielinsky, Dobroliubov, Cherny-shevsky, etc., and Lenin, Stalin and (above all) the souls they hold sway over, there is an abyss. Their spiritual texture is completely different. The anti-religious psychology of the Com-munists is one of victorious and triumphant offence and revenge, which pay off their scores and get their own back. The psychology of the victorious triumphant " proletariat " is one of compensation for former humiliation. That is precisely how Marx lays down his doctrine of the proletariat's messianic vocation. It is the most oppressed class in capitalist society, and it makes up for this by being conscious of its messianic vocation to set mankind free, its mighty power that is to come. The most remarkable modern social theorist, de Man, very rightly interprets Marx's teaching on the great mission of the proletariat in the spirit of Adler's psychology : the working class suffers from humiliation and social inferiority and makes up for it by nursing the idea of a higher vocation, so as to satisfy its longing for superiority.

The old anti-religious psychology of Russian Nihilism still had religious and even orthodox roots, that fed on the experience of sinfulness and guilt, though in a perverted way. The new is already quite severed from them : its spiritual mainspring is different. The anti-religious psychology of militant atheism is determined by a desire to dominate and wield power. It is an undeniable psychological fact that man is better able to bear the trial of persecution than that of triumph. One sees it in the history of Christianity. Christians nobly bore the trial of persecution and became martyrs ; and to-day we see the same thing in Russia—the Orthodox Church is glorious in her martyrs. But Christians have not borne the trial of triumph well ; they easily become persecutors. And the fact that they did so when they were in power was a scandal that led men to abandon the faith and become atheists. There was a time when men suffered persecution for atheism and the right to unbelief; they were thrown into prison and burnt at the stake. But in the hour of their triumph atheism and unbelief become persecutors, imprisoning and shooting faithful Christians. Russian atheism was born as something oppressed that rebels against the injustice and

34

evil of the world ; it rejected God because the world is evil, unjust and full of the sufferings of innocent people. Yet when it triumphed it became a persecutor, created a new injustice, producing evil and causing an immeasurable amount of suffering. Nihilism grew up in pure ascetic souls that sought for truth and justice. But now it is transformed ; it becomes amoral no longer in theory only but in actual life ; it grants free play to the evil instincts and rejects the justice in whose name it denied God. It is a fatal psychological process. In accordance with the Russian spiritual type, it was not so much the scientific as the messianic elements of Marxism that dominated in Russian Communism : the idea of the proletariat as the liberator and organiser of mankind, the bearer of a higher truth and a higher justice. But that messianic idea is militant, aggressive, pugnacious and domineering : the idea of exultant strength. There is no room here for the victimised, passive, all-suffering elements of old Russian messianic consciousness. The proletariat Messiah is not at all a suffering victim ; he is a victor, a world-organiser, a condenser of strength. That is, of course, above all an idea and not an empirical fact. Russia is a land of peasants ; the factory proletariat is an insignificant portion of the Russian people, and the

Revolution has not at all increased that messianic class. But an idea, a myth, is a tremendous moving force in history, and has proved to be such in Russia also. It has created a completely new soul-formation, in which suffering and sympathy, sacrifice and asceticism are crushed out by power and domination, strength and organisation. And this is the outcome of it ; the fact that the idea of God is driven out of man's consciousness in no way leads to man and the things of man being finally freed and finding their self-expression ; the result is that certain strange inhuman or superhuman forces appear in this consciousness and begin to oppress him. That is, from our point of view, an extraordinarily interesting and important psychological process.

iv

A fundamental fact in anti-religious psychology is the appearance in the human soul of idols and idolatry. Man is by his nature a religious being, and the soul of man cannot live empty of religion. Veneration and adoration of something higher cannot be torn from the human soul ; man cannot live without a relation to something superhuman. Only a superhuman principle can make up the idea of man itself. That is a fundamental truth of anthropology which must be admitted quite apart from various forms of religious belief. Now, when faith in a true living God fails, and the very idea of God is pushed out of man's consciousness, the images of false gods arise in his soul and religious worship is paid to them. Man has a tendency to idolatry that cannot be uprooted ; he has a capacity for turning absolutely anything, every kind of value, into an idol. He makes an idol of knowledge, or art, or the State, or nationality, or morality, or social justice and organisation. And to all these idols, behind which are hidden genuine values, man pays divine worship. Idolatry always makes use of undoubted values and goods, but they are spoilt and corrupted by it as the result of a violation of man's spiritual harmony. It always employs man's former religious psychology, directing to its own service all his store of religious energy, accumulated in human souls by positive religious processes.

Without a religious soul-formation devotion to any ideal would be impossible ; man could not sacrifice himself in the service of any idea, even atheistic. Absolute egoism will never succeed among men, and least of all will it succeed among Russian Nihilists and revolutionaries. Idealistic atheism always means essentially the adoption of some form of idolatry, for complete emptiness of soul can only lead to suicide. If the Communists succeeded in uprooting every form of faith from the human soul they would destroy faith in Communism— the capacity for making sacrifices in virtue of the Communist idea and of consecrating all one's energy to it.

Communism comes forward claiming to be a new religion, and it requires great stores of religious energy and great strength of religious faith if it is to be put in practice. And precisely because Communism is itself a religion it persecutes all religions and will have no religious toleration. Communistic atheism has nothing in common with laicism and liberalism. It looks upon itself as the only true religion and will suffer no other to live alongside of it. It demands religious adoration of the proletariat as the chosen people of God ; it deifies a social collectivity called to supplant God and man. The social collectivity is the one and only criterion of moral judgments and acts ; it contains and expresses all justice and truth. Communism creates a new morality which is neither Christian nor humanitarian. It has its orthodox theology and sets up its own cult (the cult of Lenin, for instance), its own symbols, its own feasts, its " red baptisms " and " red funerals." It has its own dogmatic system, obligatory for all, and its catechism ; it exposes heresies and excommunicates heretics. This religious character of Communism finds a congenial breeding ground in the religious psychology and character of the Russian people. The Russian people are passing from one mediæval period into another, after experiencing the renaissance only in its small upper class. The workman is not at all inclined to pass from Christian faith to enlightened rationalism and scepticism ; he is more inclined to go over to a new faith and a new idol-worship. Russian idealistic Communists (and the Soviet order depends entirely on them) are as believing in spiritual outlook as were the old Russian Nihilists, although their faith is now connected with different emotions and longings. Communists are by no means sceptics, and that is why the sceptical people of the West find them so difficult to understand. Real fanaticism is always a product of idol-worship. Christian fanaticism also was the result of idolatry within Christianity, of an idolatrous perversion of the Faith. And Communism is fanatical in so far as it is idolatrous, in so far as it turns relative social values into absolute ones. That is what idol-worship always does.

39

Nihilism, seen from one side, is a desolation, a turning of everything into nothing ; every relative value and benefit of culture is rejected and exterminated. But, on the other hand, it always proceeds to turn some relative values and benefits into something absolute, to deify something or other, to give divine honours to some unworthy object that is utterly devoid of divine attributes. Without that, its pathos and the self-devotion of its convinced adepts would be impossible. Russian Nihilism and atheism took on the features of that religious maximalism which is innate in the Russian character. The Russian soul, having lost the Christian faith, hankered after salvation, the saving of the people, of humanity and the world from evil and suffering. The Russian revolutionary of the twentieth century did not believe in the Saviour ; but he considered *himself* to be a saviour and a victim—that is just the pathos of his martyrdom. The Russian revolutionary accepted sacrifice and martyrdom, but he did not accept or understand the mystery of the Cross. The quest of salvation, understood either religiously or socially, is so characteristic of the Russian soul that it continually falls into doubt as to its right to cultural creation. That sort of doubt was experienced by Gogol and Tolstoy in a particularly acute way.

The ancient Russian messianic idea goes on living in the deep spiritual layers of the Russian people. But in the conscious mind its formula changes, the thing " in the name " of which it acts ; the messianic idea rises out of the collective unconsciousness of the people's life and takes on another name. Instead of the monk Philothey's Third Rome we get Lenin's Third International. It takes on Marxist clothes and Marxist symbolism, and adopts the characteristics of the Russian messianic idea ; the vocation of the Russian people is worked into it. The international and the Russian national type are so intertwined that it is difficult to distinguish them. Internationalism appears as the national Russian vocation and takes on the character of the Russian idea. The same psychological springs are at work.

Marxian Communism aims at the complete rationalisation of life, but it is itself under the influence of the Russian irrational element, collective and unconscious. Anti-religious propaganda adopts quite unrational forms ; a burning idolatrous fanaticism enters into it. Quasi-scientific arguments against faith drawn from popular pamphlets take on the nature of a fanatical faith. Already in Russian Nihilism science was never a wholly objective research ; it became an idol, an object of religious faith.

We see the same thing in Russian Communism. Scientific theories, sometimes of the most doubtful kind, become like battle-cries. Marxism itself, of which the Communist masses have a very rudimentary knowledge, is a religious symbolism, the banner of an army in battle, not a scientific theory. It is the same with Darwinism, the mechanistic explanation of life, and so on. If you are a Darwinian you are on the side of the working class and are numbered among the elect. If you believe in Lamarck you must be on the side of the exploiters, the *bourgeoisie;* you are thrown into prison and perish there. If you are a mechanist you belong to the chosen people, the saved ; but if you are a vitalist you are excommunicated and death awaits you.

Russian Communists are suspicious and hostile to the progress of modern physics ; they see in the great contemporary discoveries of physical science a *bourgeois* reaction unfavourable to materialism. They call Einstein and Planck representatives of *bourgeois* science—even of clericalism. It is obvious that all this has no relation to objective scientific knowledge. Marxism, for Russian Communists, represents something quite different from what it means to German Socialists. The so-called Russian *Mensheviks* (Social Democrats) are also Marxists, and more consequent ones for that matter. But their Marxism does not save them ; it has not the character of a religious creed, it is not capable of engendering an inverted theocracy.

It is psychologically interesting that the Communists' faith, which worships as its object the mighty collectivity of the future, feeds not so much on positive as on negative feelings. Communism cannot exist, it cannot be pathetic and intense, without an enemy to inspire it with loathing and spite. It is something very like what is felt by the dualistic, Manichean religious type. The elect of the messianic Communist faith are unable to bear sin and repentance ; evil is entirely attributed to an evil god which is called either " the world-wide *bourgeoisie* " or " world-wide imperialism," or " world-wide counter-revolution," and so forth. The world is always divided into two halves, two camps, one of which contains nothing but light, and the other nothing but darkness. Idolatry encourages this sort of dualism.

I leave aside here the point that Communism suggests a great deal of fruitful matter of thought as regards the social reform of human society, the curing of the contradictions, injustices and evils in our capitalist society of the nineteenth and twentieth centuries. That is not now my theme ; I am dealing not with

43

the social question, but with a psychological question. And what I want to point out is that the anti-religious psychology of Communism is a religious psychology turned inside-out.

In spite of the enormous psychological changes wrought in the Russian soul by the Revolution, its fundamental psychical formation remains the same as before. It was built up by Orthodoxy and it is still preserved, although the Orthodox faith has disappeared and is fought against. Ascetic denial of history and culture adopt the form of Nihilist denial of historical succession and Nihilist destruction of cultural values. Eschatological feeling and the obsession of the super-mundane take the form of man's caring for nothing on earth except the Last Judgment of social revolution and the City that is to come—the perfect Communist society. Religious absolutism and maximalism become denial of relativity, denial of the gradual measured process of historical labour. These psychological features—perversions of the Orthodox ascetic doctrine on life—are already found in the Russian Nihilists, Bielinsky, Dobroliubov, Chernyshevsky, Pisarev ; in the anarchist Bakunin ; and in another way, under a religious banner, in Tolstoy. The same features, in a completely different social atmosphere, are passed on to the more idealistic Communists—

the fanatics of Communism, not its business men. The same spiritual energy that flowed in the service of God flows in that of idols.

Consciousness is changed, yet the subconscious basis would seem to be identical. But the great difference between the service of God and the service of an idol is that a man who serves God is spiritually nourished by grace, whereas the servant of an idol has no such nourishment. An idol has no spiritual food to give and no grace to send down; it is created by a misguided application of spiritual energy, and in its service the soul remains shut up in itself, self-centred, with no outlet to superhuman realities. That is the fatal side of the worship of false gods. Religious psychology remains, only religious ontology is lacking. Anti-religious psychology in the Russian people often bears traces of a religious faith that has not disappeared. The Russian peasant in Dostoievsky's story who took the Blessed Sacrament and shot at It, dealt with It none the less as something holy. Sacrilege always presupposes some sort of belief in sanctity, otherwise it loses all its meaning; one cannot commit sacrilege to an ordinary piece of matter. And as a matter of fact the sacrilegious element plays a large part in the Communist's anti-religious propaganda. The man who com-

45

mits sacrilege not only makes a mockery of what others deem holy, he himself enters into a special relationship with the sacred objects he mocks.*

* * * *

In conclusion, I should like to recapitulate my version of the fundamental moving forces in anti-religious psychology, the pathos of atheism. It cannot be better studied than in Russian psychology. Anti-religious psychology is constituted above all as ·the result of the human soul's inability to bear the experience of evil and suffering, personal and social; it gives in under the scandal and temptation implied by the problem of theodicy—the justification of God. The conflict of religious faith with reason and science is a secondary matter, often a mere pretext for unbelief, used by the soul to convince itself of the rightness and purity of its unbelief. When a man tells himself and others that he would like to believe, but that scientific honesty and conscientiousness do not permit of his doing so, he is deceiving himself. In reality it means that his faith has not stood the trial of life, experienced by him outside the sphere of knowledge. But faith never disappears for good and all. It is trans-

* I may add that alongside of anti-religious propaganda in Soviet Russia there is also a religious revival, a re-birth of the persecuted suffering Church.

46

formed, it goes on existing in another shape ; it can be applied to the very reason and science which are used for its rejection.

The great Russian genius, Dostoievsky, had an admirable insight into the psychology and logic of atheism, especially Russian atheism, and did more than any other to throw light on them. He saw the primary source of unbelief to consist in experience of the phenomenon of suffering, yet without acceptance of the meaning of suffering—that is, of the Cross. And the fundamental Christian answer to the anti-religious revolt against suffering to be that God Himself, the Son of God, suffered, so that ever since then to suffer is to bear the Cross.

II

THE RELIGION OF COMMUNISM

i

MEN's attitude as regards Communism has been, up till now, rather emotional than intellectual. The psychological atmosphere has been very unfavourable to an understanding of the ideological world in which Communism moves. Among Russian emigrants it has roused a passionate emotional reaction such as one might expect from wounded people ; there are too many who, on being asked what Communism is, could answer, " My own shattered life and unhappy lot." In Western Europe men's attitude is characterised either by *bourgeois* fright and the *bourgeois* reaction of the capitalist world, or by the superficial and irresponsible toying with Bolshevism (a snobbish fad, for the most part) indulged in by some intellectuals. But hardly anyone has taken the ideology of Communism, the Communist *faith*, seriously.

The most remarkable of Russian philosophers in the nineteenth century, a Christian philosopher, Vladimir Solovyev, once said that to defeat what is false in Socialism one must recognise what is true in it. The same must be said of Communism, which is one of the extreme forms of Socialism. In Communism there is a great untruth, an anti-Christian untruth, but it also contains much truth, and even many truths. In Communism there are many truths which one might formulate in a whole series of paragraphs, and only one untruth ; but that untruth is so enormous that it outweighs all the truths and spoils them.

Communism should have a very special significance for Christians, for it is a reminder and denouncement of an unfulfilled duty, of the fact that the Christian ideal has not been achieved. Christian justice has not worked itself out fully in life, and in virtue of the mysterious ways of Divine Providence the forces of evil have undertaken the task of realising social justice. That is the spiritual meaning of all revolutions, their mysterious " dialectics." Christian " good " has become too conventional and rhetorical, and so the carrying out of certain elements of that " good " which is proclaimed in theory but very inadequately achieved in practice, is undertaken in a spirit of terrible reaction against Christianity. The sin and baseness of Christians, or, rather, of false Christians, have shut off and darkened the light of

Christian revelation. Throughout almost all its later history, the Christian world has been infected by a sorry duality; Christians have lived, so to speak, in two different rhythms, the religious rhythm of the Church, governing a limited number of days and hours in their life, and the unreligious rhythm of the world, governing a greater number. The greater part of their life has not been enlightened and sanctified by the Truth of Christ. The most unjustified and unenlightened aspect of it has been economic life, social life, which has been abandoned to its own law. Economic life in capitalist societies is not subjected to any higher religious and moral principle. Marx was right when he said that capitalist society is an anarchical one. Its collective life is determined by the free play of private interests, and there is nothing more opposed to the spirit of Christianity than the spirit of a capitalist society. It is not by mere chance that the epoch of capitalism has coincided with abandonment of Christianity and a weakening of Christian spiritual idealism. And the idea of Communism, which in our day oppresses and persecutes all religions and all churches, is of religious and even Christian origin. It was not always materialist and atheist; in the past it had in it a religious and spiritual note. It must be

remembered that the first Communist, the first
to trace the outline of the Communist Utopia,
was Plato ; that there was a primitive Christian
Communism, founded on the Gospel ; that
there existed a religious type of Communism
in the Middle Ages and at the time of the
Reformation ; that Thomas More, the author
of the *Utopia*, is numbered by the Catholic
Church among the Blessed ; that the Communist and Socialist movements of the early
nineteenth century in France were of a spiritual
and even religious character, though vague and
indefinite. The very word " Communism "
comes from communion, commonness, mutual
participation, and such a spiritual community
between men presupposes that they partake of
some single, higher source of life—God. Only
in God and in Christ is real communion among
men attainable ; brotherhood is only possible
under one and the same Father. It is true that
modern Communists aim at obtaining community by an exterior, mechanical, obligatory
organisation of society.* But the idea itself—
communion, sharing among men—that is,
Communism in the deeper sense of the word—
is the great eternal dream of mankind.

* The German sociologist Tönnies draws a fruitful
distinction between *Gesellschaft* and *Gemeinschaft*, but he
only speaks in terms of naturalist sociology.

The tragedy is that materialistic Communism is easier to achieve than Christian Communism. One can attempt to bring it into being by means of violence and imposition, without taking into account men's spiritual freedom and sinfulness. By such means spiritual community is unattainable, yet it is possible to create a new organisation of society. But Christianity recognises spiritual freedom and therefore it cannot believe in a forcible organisation of community. When Christendom attempted to organise it in the form of mediæval theocracy, ignoring liberty, it broke up and the design was condemned to failure. Christianity recognises the inherent value of human personality, and is incapable of organising a society in which personality is humiliated and denied. Materialistic Communism rejects the value and meaning of human personality, and so its task is lighter. But when Communists accuse Christianity of not having realised itself in actual life and freed humanity from evil and suffering, they fail to see and understand the most important thing of all—the freedom of the human spirit, and the impossibility of organising a perfect society by external, mechanical, forcible means, and of doing away with sin.

It is, however, true that some limit must be set to the prevalence of sin in social life, and that

Christians must strain their wills towards the transfiguration of society in the spirit of Christ. It is nothing but a hypocritical fallacy when conservative *bourgeois* Christianity argues that to transfigure and improve human society and introduce greater justice into it is impossible, because of the sinfulness of human nature. In reality the attempt to do so is not imperative because we are optimistic about human nature after the manner of Rousseau, but precisely because we are pessimistic about it and consider that some order must be set up that will put a limit to the outbreak of sin in social life. It is the *bourgeois* ideology born of capitalism which has been optimistic, and believed in a natural harmony arising out of the conflict of private interests. Communism is possible, and universal Communism may one day be possible, not at all as the result of human nature's sinlessness, but precisely because of its sinfulness. And society will be radically rearranged by the forces of *sin*, if truth does not trouble to do the rearrangement. Utopias are much more capable of being carried out than has been so far believed. Sin itself can very well realise a Utopia. But the guilt and responsibility for the evil which that will involve will fall both on " good " turned into mere rhetoric, and on "the good" who were capable of

54

judging others but no longer capable of judging themselves. Communism, in its sinister and Godless form, is the fate of so-called " Christian " societies and at the same time a reminder, the judgment which those societies did not want to pass on themselves and which will therefore be passed upon them. And that is why it is so difficult to distinguish, in Communism, between truth and untruth.

The honour of having discovered Communism does not belong to the Russian people ; they received it from the West. But they undoubtedly have the honour of its first incarnation in actual life. And so we come to the question of what constitutes the attractiveness of Communism, why it is so infectious, why its ideas were victorious in the Russian Revolution, and why the Communist creed moves masses and creates enthusiasm.* Now, it is impossible to understand that if Communism is considered merely as a political and economic phenomenon and subjected to rational criticism from the standpoint of political economy. Communism, both as a theory and as a practice, is not only a social phenomenon, but also a

* It is only as regards the very first stage of the Revolution that one can explain the popularity of Communism by the fact that it flatters the masses, connives in their instincts and interests, and calls upon them to " rob the robbers."

55

spiritual and religious phenomenon. And it is formidable precisely as a *religion*. It is as a religion that it opposes Christianity and aims at ousting it; it gives in to the temptations Christ refused, the changing of stones into bread and the kingdom of this world.

As a social system, Communism could be neutral towards religion. But, like every religion, it carries with it an all-embracing relation to life, decides all its fundamental questions, and claims to give a meaning to everything; it has its dogmas and its dogmatic morals, publishes its catechisms, has even the beginnings of its own cult; it takes possession of the whole soul and calls forth enthusiasm and self-sacrifice. Unlike most political parties, it will not admit secularised politics, divorced from an all-embracing *Weltanschauung*. Its un-human activity is, as it were, an explosion of religious energy stored up in the human soul by a lengthy religious process. If the Communists succeeded, by anti-religious propaganda, in finally tearing from the heart of man all religious feeling, faith, and readiness for self-sacrifice in the name of faith, they would make faith in Communism impossible too; they would put an end to their own existence and nobody would be left who was willing to make sacrifices for the sake of the Communist idea.

Thus even in the name of an anti-Christian idea they make use of the Christian formation of the soul, the Christian capacity for faith and sacrifice. There is no denying the deplorable fact that Christians themselves, in the *bourgeois* period of history, have given proof of much less energy and power of self-sacrifice than the Communists. The figures of the great saints and ascetics were pushed back into the remote past ; Christianity has been going through an unheroical, decadent period and thereby preparing the successes of Communism. It is an undeniable fact, quite impossible to conceal, that the youth of Soviet Russia are sincerely and unconditionally fired with enthusiasm for Communism. We see it in the energy which the Communist youth voluntarily expends for the realisation of the Five Years' Plan.

Theoretically, Communism is Marxism ; Marxism is the obligatory creed of the Communist party. Can Marxism, a doctrine well known in the West, help one to understand the attractiveness of the Communist idea ? But Marxism is also the basis of the German Social Democratic Party, in which one can perceive very little enthusiasm and abnegation ; it is a business-like, moderate party, very unlike a religious movement, and by no means fanatical. The complication and difficulty of understand-

57

ing Russian Communism lies partly in the fact
that it is at once an international worldwide
phenomenon and a national Russian one. In
it the rationalistic doctrine of Marxism has been
broken up by the irrational Russian element
and deformed. Here we find something of a
process that is repeated in all great revolutions.
Revolutions are brought on by irrational
elemental forces generated in the obscure subconscious life of the people ; and yet at the
same time they always aim at rationalising life
and take their stand on some rational doctrine
that becomes their conventional war-cry. The
French Revolution, for example, drew its inspiration from the rationalistic " enlightened "
philosophy of the eighteenth century, but the
active forces in it were demoniacal and irrational. And the Russian Communist Revolution
is absolutely intent on rationalising life completely so that every irrational element and
every mystery is utterly driven out of it ; yet it
also is moved, and moved with the utmost
intensity, by irrational demoniacal elements,
for which the rationalistic doctrine serves
merely as a conventional system of symbols.
It is not at all the rationalistic, objective,
scientific elements of Marxism that are at work
in Russian Communism, but the mythological
and religious elements. This curious combina-

58

tion of the rational and irrational element in the Russian Revolution actually gave rise to a legend, which is popular among the simple people, peasants, workmen and middle classes, that there is a distinction between Bolshevism and Communism. Bolshevism is held to be a purely Russian thing, a popular thing, an outbreak of revolution on the part of the Russian people, whereas Communism is a foreign thing that has come in from outside and bound the popular Revolution with the chains of rational organisation. And there is a real distinction between the irrational and rational elements in the Revolution, corresponding to that conventional distinction between the two terms. A revolutionary idea always includes some rational element, and in this case it is taken from Marxism. The question is: What is there in Marxism that can sweep on and inspire the masses into a vast and powerful movement?

ii

At the basis of Marxism lies the theory of economic or historical materialism, according to which the entire process of history and social life is determined by economics, by the development of material productive forces, and by the various forms of production and exchange.

59

Economics are the " basis " of all life, its primordial authentic reality, whereas all the rest, all " ideology," spiritual life, religious belief, philosophy, morals, art, all the culture which man considers to be the flower of life, is a 'superstructure," an epiphenomenon, a fallacious and illusory reflection in man's consciousness of the real economic processes. Marx is not the only thinker who has insisted on the overwhelming importance of economics, that is, of the degree of mastery over the elemental forces of Nature which socially organised man has reached ; other historians and Utopian Socialists did so before him—Saint Simon, for example, who anticipated Marx in many respects. But Marx made the idea into a system of universal economic metaphysics, and he combined his economic metaphysics or ontology (*i.e.*, his teaching on the nature of being, on the ultimate reality) with the doctrine of the class struggle, which is the special " discovery," or rather " revelation," of his own genius. This last had also been spoken of before him by a more modest science, history ; but the idea of the proletariat's messianic vocation belongs to Marx alone. The theory of economic materialism by itself could not be an inspiration for anyone : a doctrine according to which all human life is determined by economic processes is rather a sad one, apt to make a man drop his hands in despondency. But Marx by no means limits himself to that unhappy truth. He is pessimistic about the past, which is seen by him in its very darkest colours, but he is an optimist as regards the future, in which he sees nothing but the brightest. Marx and Engels teach that mankind can jump from the realm of necessity into that of freedom. It is only the past that has been a realm of necessity determined by economics. The future will bring in the realm of freedom ; social reason will finally vanquish all the irrational, elemental forces of Nature and society, and social man will become the mighty king of the universe.

In prodigious contradiction with his own materialism, Marx believes in the " dialectics " inherited from Hegel. He believes that the " dialectic process " will inevitably lead through evil to good, through the meaningless to the triumph of meaning. Hegel's dialectics are connected with the idea of a universal Logos : in them the Logos, the Meaning of the universe, must infallibly triumph. The world-process, for Hegel, is " dialectic " because it is a " logical " process, a self-revelation of Intelligence ; dialectics of its parts are only possible as the result of their being absorbed into the logical heart of the whole. There is not the slightest possibility of translating such panlogical dialectics into the language of materialism, for matter is ignorant of the Logos and the triumph of Meaning. Yet Marx lays down a system of materialistic dialectics, and he is able to do so because he introduces the panlogical principle into the heart of matter itself, into the material economic process. He believes that that process will lead through the struggle of contradictory forces into the triumph of Meaning, Reason, Logos—to the realm of freedom, to Order, to victory over the necessity introduced by the elemental irrational forces of Nature. A mad belief: for it remains incomprehensible why the elemental, material, economic process does not lead to the complete triumph of meaninglessness, slavery and darkness ; such a process is by nature irrational and can guarantee no triumph of reason. Yet Marx looks ahead to a perfect Communist society which will be the very incarnation of reason, justice and order ; there will be nothing irrational, nothing unjust in it ; life will be rationalised once and for ever—the triumph of panlogism. In Marx we find an astounding combination : an acute feeling and consciousness of a furious struggle between demoniacal, irrational forces in history (they remind one of the violent forces which Jakob Böhme perceived struggling at opposite poles in the life of the universe), and an absolute conviction that reason, meaning, justice, order and organisation will be victorious in social life. Such an inconceivable combination of demoniacal social irrationalism and social " panlogism," such a blackening of the past and brilliant concept of the future, are attractive features of his system. Moreover, the brilliant future is inevitable, the realm of freedom is pre-determined. In the future the elemental economic principle will have no more power over the life of human societies, which will be determined by social reason in its victory over every other element. The dialectics of the material process lead infallibly to the Kingdom of God on earth (but without God), to the realm of freedom, justice and power. By itself the theory of economic materialism would be unable to enlist enthusiasm ; it would merely remain one out of many scientific hypotheses. What does rouse enthusiasm is Marx's messianic faith. It finds its complete expression in the idea of the proletariat's messianic vocation. The aspect of Marxism which looks forward to the future Socialist society and to the great mission of the proletariat has nothing in common with science —it is a faith, " the substance of things to be

63

hoped for, the evidence of things that appear not." Marx's " proletariat " and his perfect Socialist society are " invisible things," an object of faith. Here we are in contact with a *religious* idea.

According to Marx, the basis of the historical process is not only economics, the development of material productive forces (that alone could not rouse much feeling), but also the class-struggle. All the violence of Marxism is founded on the notion of that struggle. It is its subjective aspect ; its scale of values is connected with it. And undoubtedly Marx's very idea of a class is " axiological," conceived in terms of intrinsic value. The distinction between " proletariat " and " *bourgeoisie* " unwittingly coincides with that between " good " and " evil." In his conscious thought Marx remains a complete amoralist, but his teaching on the class struggle is moralistic through and through—with a curious negative kind of moralism. There is no good or justice, but there *is* evil and injustice. And they arouse indignation and hatred. He believes in an original sin lying at the basis of human society, the sin of one man's exploiting another, which always takes the shape of class exploiting class. Marx wants to give " exploiting " a purely economic character : he combines the idea

64

with the theory of an additional price extorted from the workers and appropriated by the exploiting classes. But, philosophically speaking, it is obvious that the idea cannot be purely economic : it is necessarily ethical. When we say that exploiting is practised, we make a moral judgment. If the amoralist denial of the distinction between good and evil is accepted, it is incomprehensible why the exploiting of man by man should call forth revolt and condemnation as an injustice. Marxism is an extreme form of determinist philosophy, despising every moral appreciation. For it, moral freedom is non-existent. Nevertheless it implies at its basis the idea of original sin—an original sin which infects all the history of the world, all classes of society, and disfigures all human beliefs and every form of ideology.

The sin of exploitation cuts off all possibility of apprehending truth and creates an illusory doctrine to maintain and justify itself. Economic realities receive an illusory expression in men's consciousness—such is Marx's fundamental idea. He is forced to regard as illusory all former ideas and beliefs. In their fundamental principle Marx and Freud are not far apart. Both aim at unmasking the illusory nature of man's conscious life, its deception and untruth ;

and behind that illusion, deception and untruth of consciousness they see certain unconscious impulses, which Marx holds to be economic class interests and exploiting, and Freud *libido*, sexual impulses and the complexes they give rise to. Marx has not yet discovered the *sub-*conscious mind ; his psychology is rationalistic ; but he aims continually at unmasking the lie of consciousness, of conscious ideas and theories. Now, a man who unmasks the lie and illusion of consciousness must himself be conscious of having the truth and know by what means truth can vanquish untruth, and reality defeat illusion. And so Marx believes that the historical moment has come when truth is to be at last revealed. At last he has succeeded in unmasking illusion and revealing truth, in finding the key to the understanding of the world's history, in discovering the secret of the life of human societies. Truth is revealed to him, light enlightens the darkness that engulfed all the past, because in his person the class which is called to be the liberator of mankind thinks and perceives the truth. Relativity is overcome ; proletarian truth is no mere reflex of economics, but an absolute truth. Every social class has been infected in various ways by the sin of exploiting and therefore shut off from the truth. The very organisation of society on

66

a class basis reflected man's weakness, his dependence on the elemental forces of Nature and of society itself; for a society founded on the class struggle is enslaved to irrational forces and has no power over its own self. Religious beliefs merely reflect the weakness and helplessness of man against those natural forces, the low development of material productive forces, and man's dependence on his neighbour, man's slavery. And then capitalist society takes shape. Marx considers it to be society's wickedest and most unjust form, in which one class exploits another to the utmost limit. Yet, at the same time, such a society develops mankind's productive forces, generates power, and brings into life a new class unknown to past history, the proletariat.

The proletariat is the only class that is innocent of the original sin of exploitation. It is the class that produces all the material treasures and goods on which human society lives. It is exploited and crushed : the most disinherited class, deprived of the means of production, living in servile dependence on Capital. But in it there grows up a force, a collective power, that will be revealed when capitalist society has crashed to its doom. The proletariat is a messianic class ; its vocation is to be the liberator of all mankind, it is even identified with true humanity, it is already not merely a class, for it is outgrowing the society which includes it as a class. Truth is being revealed to it and it is already introducing justice in virtue of its social position. The messianic concept of the proletariat includes the freeing of the oppressed, that is, the achievement of social justice, and the attainment of might and power by a socially organised humanity. With the proletariat's victory social rationalism will utterly triumph and master the irrational forces of the world. Its victory will bring with it the final rationalisation of life, a final regulation and ordering; everything irrational, obscure and mysterious will be banished from life. The anarchy which Marx perceived in capitalist society will come to an end. The proletariat is clothed in all the virtues.

Now, it is perfectly clear that Marx's " proletariat " is not the empirical working class which we observe in actual life. It is a mythical idea, not an objective reality. Marx's proletarian myth resembles J. J. Rousseau's democratic myth, but its content is radically different, for proletarian Communism is opposed on principle to formal democracy. The myth of the proletariat has an active force, it is intensely dynamic and explosive. The " proletariat " category conceived by Marx is above all

68

axiological, appreciative. The "proletariat" is a mythical notion and, at the same time, the supreme value, good and justice—a positive power. The distinction between "proletariat" and "*bourgeoisie*" does not record an empirical fact observed as such in actual existence ; it is, first and foremost, an appreciation, a judgment. There is a strong axiological element in the whole Marxian theory of the class struggle. Marx would never have arrived at his concept of a class and especially of the proletariat, if he had not introduced into it an estimate of loftiness and baseness, "good" and "evil." For Marxism, like every extreme revolutionary ideology, contains an unconscious survival of dualistic Manichean tendencies, of the sharp opposition between the kingdom of a good god and that of an evil god. That dualism will be overcome with the victory of the proletariat.

But the most important aspect of Marx's teaching concerning the proletariat's messianic vocation is the fact that he applied to the proletariat the characteristics of God's chosen people. Marx was a Jew ; he had abandoned the faith of his fathers, but the messianic expectation of Israel remained in his subconsciousness. The subconscious is always stronger than the conscious, and for him the proletariat is a new Israel, God's chosen people, the liberator and builder of an earthly kingdom that is to come. His proletarian Communism is a secularised form of the ancient Jewish chiliasm. A Chosen Class takes the place of the chosen people. It was impossible to reach such a notion by means of science. It is an idea of a religious kind. Here we have the very marrow of the Communist religion. For a messianic consciousness is surely always of ancient Hebrew origin ; it is foreign to Hellenic thought. And such is Russian messianic consciousness also. Messianic feeling, messianic consciousness, imparts an enormous power ; it inspires, calls forth enthusiasm, incites to self-sacrifice. And it is this which inspires the Socialist Labour movement. If it has grown weak in the Socialist Democratic movement, if that movement has taken on a *bourgeois* tone, in Communism such messianic consciousness is very strong indeed. Communists have an acute feeling that a fatal hour of history has arrived, a worldwide catastrophe, after which a new era will begin for mankind. Only such a feeling as that can make their unhuman energy and activity possible. The Marxist theory of a catastrophe of capitalist society is nothing else but faith in the certain coming of the Last Judgment. Revolutionary Communism has a very strong eschatological element in it. The time and hour are nigh, a gap in time is approaching. That is what the chief theorist of " religious socialism " in Germany, Tillich, expresses by the word *Kairos* : a kind of intrusion of eternity into time. Marxism is quite incapable of expressing it in terms of its superficial materialist philosophy, but it is just what lies in its underground, its subconsciousness. And that is what its force consists in. Here lies the unwinding of the chain of determinism : a break appears in evolution, a leap from the realm of necessity into that of freedom ; history ends and superhistory begins.

In the Russian Revolution a meeting and union of two messianic consciousnesses took place, that of the proletariat and that of the Russian people. The Russian people become, as it were, identified with the proletariat, though, of course, the coincidence is by no means an objective fact. The previous essay showed the messianic feeling which for centuries possessed the Russian people. It was shown there how it suffered a tragic shock in the religious schism of the seventeenth century and took on new shapes in the extreme sects ; how it found its way into the upper cultured class of the nineteenth, among Russian writers and thinkers ; how it remained in a secularised form among the Russian revolutionaries of the nineteenth century ; and how it is found in an extreme form in the anarchist Bakunin. Dostoievsky expressed the same messianic feeling in his idea of the Russians as the " God-bearing " people. When K. Leontyev lost faith in a positive religious vocation of the Russian people, he began to believe that it was destined to give birth to anti-Christ : in other words it is messianic, but in an evil sense. And in its latest form, not only secularised but even made completely Godless, Russian messianism appears in Bolshevism, in Communism. Russian Communism believes that Light will come out of the East, that the light of the Russian Revolution will illuminate the *bourgeois* darkness of the West. The Russian people did not achieve their ancient dream of Moscow, the Third Rome. Imperial Russia was very far from resembling a Third Rome. But, instead of the Third Rome, they have established the Third International. And in that Third International a sinister combination has taken place between the Russian national messianic idea and the international proletarian messianic idea. That is why the Russian Revolution, inspired by the proletarian international idea, is none the less a Russian national revolution. The Communist religion is not of Russian origin, but it has been reflected in a peculiar way in the Russian religious type, which is characterised by an eschatological expectation of the advent of God's Kingdom on earth.

iii

What is true in Communism ? One can lay down a whole series of assertions in which truth is on its side. First of all there is its negative truth, its criticism of the falsehood of *bourgeois* capitalist civilisation, of its contradictions and diseases. Then there is the truth of its denouncement of a degenerate, decadent pseudo-Christianity, adapted to the interests of the *bourgeois* epoch of history. But there is also positive truth in its scheme for organising and regulating the economic life of society, on which men's lives depend, and which can no longer be abandoned to the free play of individual interests and arbitrariness. The idea of methodically planning out the norms of economic life is, on principle, a right idea. The liberal principle of formal freedom in such matters produces enormous injustices and deprives a considerable portion of humanity of all real liberty. The truth contained in Communism is that society ought to be a working society of labourers, and that the working-classes ought to be called to play their part in history and share its culture (though it is true that Communism has not a right understanding of the qualitative hierarchy of labour). The Russian Communists who pasted up the slogan " If any man will not work, neither let him eat " on every fence in Soviet Russia probably did not suspect that those words belong to St. Paul the Apostle. Communism is right when it declares that man should not exploit man and class exploit class. Man's mastery over Nature's elements ought not to lead to the dominating of his neighbour. It is true that the dissociation of society into classes struggling against each other must be overcome, and that classes should be replaced by professions. It is true that political organs ought to represent men's real economic needs and interests, and therefore be arranged on a basis of profession and labour. That truth is connected with Communism's criticism of democracy as a form of political life. Politics should serve economics : * it is social realism that demands it. It is true that political life should go hand in hand with a complete consistent philosophy of life ; for politics without a soul, without some great idea, cannot enliven the souls of men. It is true that theory and

* In Russian Communism politics dominate economics at present, which is in flagrant contradiction with Marxism. But that is a characteristic of revolutionary dictatorship, not an ideal of normal social order.

74

practice should be united in some all-embracing entire type of culture and life. The upper cultured class, the *élite*, cannot remain detached from social life, deprived of a social basis ; it should serve the social whole. Finally, it is true that national selfishness and isolation, producing hostility and war, should be overcome by some supernational organisation of mankind.

Communism states before the whole world the great problem of its radical social reconstruction. The whole world is burning, thirsting for transformation, seeking a new and better life. The strength of Communism lies in its having a complete design for reconstructing the world's life, in which theory and practice, thought and will are at one. And in that respect it resembles the theocratic design of the Middle Ages. For Communism subjects the life of individual man to a great, worldwide, super-individual end. It goes back again to the concept of life as a service—an idea completely lost in the de-Christianised, *bourgeois* liberal epoch. Every young man feels he is building up a new world. It may very well be the building of the Tower of Babel, but it fills the life of the very least among men with something super-individual which sweeps him on and sustains him. Economics are no longer

75

a private affair, they are a world affair. Man is being forcibly freed from private life, he is reconstructing the world. Communism denies individual man, but it accepts collective man as omnipotent. Every human being is called to reconstruct the world collectively. The weight of the past, of history and tradition, which are so strong in the West, is thrown aside. It is as though the creation of the earth were beginning afresh. The very freedom of the Western nations prevents the radical reconstruction of the world ; there the preservation of the *status quo* gives a feeling of freedom, while change is felt as its violation. Nevertheless, Communism has no idea of freedom as the possibility of choice, of turning to right or left, but only as the possibility of giving full play to one's energy when once one has chosen which way to turn. Freedom of choice seems to it to be a freedom that weakens and saps energy. If one compares Soviet Russia with France, for instance, one can say that the first is a land of coercion, while the latter is one of liberty. Yet in a land of liberty it is very difficult to reform social life ; the very principle of formal freedom has become a conservative principle. That is one of the paradoxes of freedom.

The Russian Revolution has given proof of enormous vital strength. But its force cannot be entirely attributed to Communism, which is merely its conventional formula ; it is above all the vital strength of the Russian people, a force formerly held in leash and now unchained.

But the untruth in Communism is greater than its truth. It has even disfigured that truth. It is above all a spiritual, not a social falseness. What is false and terrible is the very spirit of Communism. Its spirit is the negation of spirit, the negation of the spiritual principle in man. Its untruth is its rejection of God. Everything flows from that source. Godlessness cannot go unpunished. Communism is inhuman, for denial of God leads to denial of man. Communism has not stopped midway in the transitional realm of humanism. It has denied God not in the name of man, as generally happens, but in the name of a third principle—the social collectivity, its new divinity ; and consequently it has also denied what it calls the Christian " myth," whereas Humanism did not get as far as its logical, complete rejection. For the Christian " myth " is not only about God but also about man ; it is a theandric " myth." At first men tried to get rid of only one half of it, the " myth " about God, leaving the " myth " about man intact. The idea of man's central, supreme position is a remains of the Christian " myth." Man is God's idea,

God's creation, the image and likeness of God. That constitutes his supreme dignity and absolute significance. The dialectics of the humanistic process were such that at first men denied God, but still left His image and likeness in man and based man's absolute significance on that resemblance. That is brought out with extraordinary strength and acuity in Feuerbach's anthropological philosophy. He denied God and put anthropology in the place of theology ; but man, for him, is still endowed with divine attributes. Man creates God in his own image and likeness—which is merely an inversion of the Christian truth that God created man in His. The Christian " myth " about man is kept by Feuerbach ; his philosophy is Godless, but not inhuman. The anthropological myth is still Christian in origin. Now Marx followed up Feuerbach, and adopted all the arguments of his atheism, but he went much further in his destruction of the Christian theandric " myth." He no longer has Feuerbach's faith in man as a divinity. He proclaims a doctrine that is not anthropocentric, but sociocentric or proletariocentric. His man has lost the image and likeness of God ; he is the image and likeness of society. He is entirely a product of his social surroundings, of the economics of his epoch and the class to which

78

he belongs. Man is a function of society and even, more precisely, of a class. Man does not exist ; only his class exists. And when classes have ceased to exist, man too will cease to exist ; there will only be the social collectivity, Communist society.

Such is the final result of the denial of God, of His image and likeness in man, of the spiritual principle in man. All the negative aspects of Communism follow from that. It is social idolatry. Rejection of the living God always leads to the creation of false gods. The social collectivity which receives divine honours steps into the place of both God and man. The centre of consciousness is shifted. There is no more personal conscience, personal reason, no more personal freedom. There is only collec-tive conscience, reason, freedom. A very instructive example in this connection is Trotsky's autobiography, very self-centred but also a work of great talent, which witnesses to the dramatic fate of revolutionary personality in the revolutionary collectivity. After Lenin, Trotsky is the chief creator of the Bolshevik Revolution. He is a very typical revolutionary. But he is not a genuine Communist, a Com-munist through and through. He still admits the possibility of individual opinion, individual criticism, individual initiative ; he believes in the part to be played by heroic revolutionary personalities and counts himself, of course, among their number. He does not grasp what one may call the mysticism of collectivity—the most unpleasant side of Communism.

All the untruths of Communism come from its Godlessness and inhumanity ; the falseness of the sanguinary coercion by which it wants to found social justice, the falseness of the tyranny that cannot bear man's dignity ; its admission of every conceivable means to further the end it considers as supreme and unique ; rancour, hatred and revenge as a way of obtaining perfect life, the brotherhood of men. There was a demoniacal element in Marx's teaching, which gave it its invincible dynamism. He believed that good can be produced by evil, that light can be obtained through darkness, that freedom would result from dire blind necessity. Evil must increase, darkness must thicken. That is how he understood the dialectics of the social process. The workmen's lot must grow worse in capitalist society (the *Verelendungstheorie*), the labourers must become more and more embittered and penetrated by vindicative and violent emotions. That is the basis of Marx's revolutionary messianic hope. He wants the working class, which is an empirical reality, to be saturated with proletarian consciousness.

When that happens, feelings of resentment, envy, hatred and revenge will grow up in it.

A " worker " must be distinguished from a " proletarian." A workman is a labourer, and labour is sacred ; his lot is a hard one, and must be improved, one must struggle to free the workers from slavery. But a proletarian is not simply a workman, he is a workman full of the messianic idea of the proletariat and its future power. The proletariat is not an empirical reality at all ; it is an idea. And in that aspect Marxism, which consciously professes the most naïve materialism, is an extreme idealism. It wants to subject reality to an " idea," and that " idea " coerces and cripples reality. One must not take Communism's materialist appearance too literally ; it is conventional, a mere struggle against religion and Christianity. In reality Communism is highly spiritual and idealist. Its very materialism is spiritual and idealist, matter itself hardly plays any part in it. And its spirituality is a dark, Godless spirituality. One must accuse Communists of being men of an " idea " too much, not too little. Living personality does not exist for them. No doubt Communism is characterised by an extreme obsession with economics, amounting to a perfect nightmare, which oppresses life and crushes out all its other

81

aspects. The Soviet Communist Press is filled with nothing but economics, it contains nothing else at all. But it is a very peculiar kind of economics ; they are spiritual and metaphysical economics, that take the place of God and spiritual life and reveal real being, the essence of things.

Economics are no invention of Marx, any more than materialism is. The latter he got from enlightened *bourgeois* society of the eighteenth century, the former from capitalist society of the nineteenth. But Marxism gave economics a metaphysical and even religious colouring. The messianic hope is bound up with them. The Five Years' Plan, whose prosaic object is to industrialise Russia and which, objectively, is not Socialism at all, but State capitalism, is experienced as a religious emotion. The hierarchy of values had already been spoilt by *bourgeois* capitalism, which denied the superiority of spiritual values. It had already witnessed a qualitative lowering of the level of culture ; it was a society that worshipped Mammon. And the unique importance that technical science acquires in Communist " construction " is inherited from industrial capitalist civilisation, and is often an imitation of America. But in Communism the passion for technical science assumes an ominous eschato-

logical note. Communism is torn by a fundamental contradiction ; it is inspired by a vast
idea of reconstructing the world ; it rouses
inhuman energy in men and fills them with
enthusiasm, and yet at the same time it creates
a grey, dull earthly paradise, a realm of
bureaucracy, in which everything will be
rationalised and there will be no more mystery
and infinity. Economics turn out to be man's
only province ; outside them there is no longer
any life, any being. The death-blow is given
once and for ever to the great ideas of God and
Man, and with them the whole content of
human life falls, leaving only economics and
technical science.

It is impossible to understand Communism if
one sees in it only a social system. But one can
comprehend the passionate tone of anti-religious
propaganda and persecution in Soviet Russia, if
one sees Communism as a *religion* that is striv-
ing to take the place of Christianity. Only a
religion is characterised by the claim to possess
absolute truth ; no political or economic movement can claim that. Only a religion can be
exclusive. Only a religion has a catechism
which is obligatory for everyone. Only a
religion can claim to possess the very depths of
the human soul. No political programme or
State can lay down such a claim. Communism

persecutes all religions because it is itself a religion. Recognising itself as the one true religion, it cannot suffer other false religions alongside of it. Besides, it is a religion that aims at making its way into life by force and coercion, taking no account of the freedom of the human spirit. It is the religion of the Kingdom of this world, the last and final denial of the other world, of every kind of spirituality. That is precisely the reason why its very materialism becomes spiritual and mystic. The Communist State is quite different from the ordinary lay, secularised State. It is a sacred, " theocratic " State, which takes over the functions that belong to the church. It forms men's souls, gives them an obligatory creed, demands their whole soul, exacts from them not only " what is Cæsar's " but even " what is God's." It is most important to grasp this pseudo-theocratic nature of the Communist State. Its whole structure is determined by it. It is a system of extreme social monism, in which there is no distinction between State, society and church. Therefore, such a State cannot tolerate any church alongside of it, or if it tolerates any it is only temporarily and for opportunist reasons. The old Christian theocratic State was also unable to bear any other religion or church competing with it. That was in essential contradiction with Christian spiritual freedom and so contributed to the break-up of theocracy. But communistic " theocracy " is more consistent with itself, for spiritual freedom is no part of the faith that inspires it.

Christianity has not put its truth into full living practice. It has found its realisation either in conventional formulæ or in theocracies which deliberately ignore freedom (which is the fundamental condition of any genuine realisation), or it has practised a system of duality, as in modern history, when its power has weakened. And therefore Communism has made its appearance as a punishment and a reminder, as a perversion of some genuine truth. Communism contains an eschatological element. The Apocalypse does not only signify the revelation that history is ended. There is an apocalypse within history too. The end is always nigh, time is always on the verge of eternity. The world of our day is by no means an absolutely closed world ; but there are times when that cessation of time in the presence of eternity is felt with greater acuteness. The eschatological element means not only judgment passed on history, but also judgment passed *in* history. And Communism is a judgment of that kind. The truth that refused to realise itself in beauty, in divine beauty, is carried out in ugliness.

85

Here we stand before a vitally interesting phenomenon. The Russian Communists are the first men in history who have attempted to introduce the Communist idea into real life.* But how did they enter into life, with what spiritual features, with what sort of expression on their faces ? They entered it with a look of unheard-of spiritual and moral ugliness, of unprecedented gracelessness. The grace of beauty did not light up their entry upon the scene of life. That is why Communists are so resentful ; they are irritated by the fact that they produce such an impression of indecency. Everything about them turned out to be disfigured : an ugly expression on their faces, hideous gestures, an odiously ignoble turn of mind, the monstrous atmosphere of revolutionary life in Soviet Russia. The thing has a profound ontological meaning. There may well be a great deal of social truth in Communism. I am convinced that there is. But the deformity it acquires when once that truth is put into practice means that it is mixed with a great deal of untruth, that God has stood aside from the path it has chosen for its realisation. Ugliness is always a sign of ontological corruption. For genuine, enlightened, transfigured

* Before them there had been no more than partial outbreaks of Communism.

86

being, full of grace, is beautiful. The Russian Communist Revolution has nothing of those fine theatrical gestures and splendid feats of rhetoric that marked the great French Revolution. The Russian people are not theatrical or rhetorical. Lenin wrote and spoke on purpose in an ugly coarse manner, without the slightest ornament ; it was typical of the asceticism and poverty of Russian Nihilism. Trotsky seems to be the one and only man in the Russian Revolution who is fond of fine gesture and theatrical effect, and wants to preserve the beauty which the figure of a revolutionary implies. And yet the hideousness of Russian Communists has also its positive aspect. It expresses the truth that they have abandoned truth, the untruth in their way of practising truth. Which does not mean, of course, that beauty always characterises those who oppose Communism.

iv

With what must one oppose Communism? How should one struggle against it? The way men usually oppose it and struggle against it is calculated rather to strengthen Communism than to weaken it. It gives new arguments to its defenders. For what is most terrible in it is the mixture of truth and falsehood. It cannot be opposed by any sort of Restoration, by the capitalist society and *bourgeois* civilisation of the nineteenth and twentieth centuries. Individualistic and liberal principles are already outlived; they have no more vital force left. When a relative principle claims absolute significance, what one needs to set against it is above all a real absolute principle, not some other relative principles likewise claiming absolute significance. When a time revolts against eternity, the only thing to set against it is genuine eternity itself, and not some other time which has already roused, and not without reason, a violent reaction against itself. It is no use opposing Communism with ideas; it can only be done with religious realities. Marxism has given the lie to exalted ideas as they appear in history. It is false, not because exalted ideas govern history (for the old humanism is done for), but because God exists as a tremendous reality, and strength and the last word belong to Him.

The only thing to pit against integral Communism, materialistic Communism, is integral Christianity : not rhetorical, tattered, decadent Christianity, but renascent Christianity, working out its eternal truth towards consistent life, consistent culture, consistent social justice.

The whole future of Christian societies depends on whether Christianity or, rather, Christians decisively leave off supporting capitalism and social injustice : on whether the Christian world sets to work, in the name of God and of Christ, to put into practice that justice which the Communists are now introducing in the name of a Godless collectivity, an earthly paradise. If the labouring classes have become an exceptionally favourable breeding-ground for the poison of Godlessness, if militant atheism has become nothing less than " opium for the people," the guilt must be attributed first of all by no means only to the agitators of revolutionary Socialism, but also to the Christians, to the old Christian world. It is not Christianity, of course, that is to blame, but Christians : they are too often pseudo-Christians.

Good which does not work itself into life, which has turned into conventional rhetoric so as to hide actual real evil and injustice, cannot avoid raising revolt, and righteous revolt, against its own self. The Christians of our *bourgeois* epoch of history have created most painful associations in the minds of the working-class ; they have not done Christ's mission to the souls of the oppressed and exploited a harm that can with difficulty be remedied. The situation of the Christian world face to face with Communism is not merely that of the depository of eternal and absolute truth, but also that of a guilty world, which has not practised the truth it possesses, but rather turned traitor to it. Communists do practise their truth and they can always oppose that fact to Christians. Of course, Christian truth is much harder to carry out than Communist truth. Much more, not less, is demanded of Christians than of Communists, of materialists. And if Christians carry out less, and not more, Christian truth itself is not to blame. The historical tragedy is that genuine Christianity can, apparently, never obtain complete mastery and power in this world. Mastery and power have only belonged to pseudo-Christianity. The world turns away from integral Christianity.

Meanwhile Christianity is the only basis on which a solution can be found for the painful conflict between personality and society, which Communism resolves in favour of society completely crushing personality. And it is also the only basis on which a solution can be found for the no less painful conflict between the aristocratic and democratic principles in culture, resolved by Communism in favour of completely overthrowing the aristocratic principle. On a basis of irreligion, either aristocracy oppresses and exploits democracy or democracy vulgarises the souls of men, lowers the cultural level, and destroys nobility.

Integral Christianity can accept all that is true in Communism and reject all that is false. If there is not a Christian revival in the world, a rebirth not only among the *élite* but also among the great masses of the people, atheistic Communism will conquer over the whole earth. Will that happen ? We cannot tell ; it is the secret of man's freewill. There is no reason to be very optimistic. Christianity has still to undertake the creation of a new type of sanctity among the very dregs of the world. The future belongs, whatever happens, to the working classes, to the workers ; it is inevitable, and it is just. And all depends on what their spirit will be : in whose name will they renew life, in the name of God and of Christ, of the spiritual principle in man, or in the name of Antichrist, of divinised matter, in the name of a divinised human collectivity, in which the very image of man disappears, and the human soul expires ? The Russian people have stated the problem before the whole world.

ANN ARBOR PAPERBACKS FOR THE STUDY OF COMMUNISM AND MARXISM

For a complete list of Ann Arbor Paperback titles write:

THE UNIVERSITY OF MICHIGAN PRESS / ANN ARBOR